Why did
THE HOLOCAUST
happen?

SEAN SHEEHAN

WAYLAND

First published in 2013 by Wayland

Copyright © 2011 Arcturus Publishing Limited

Wayland
Hachette Children's Books
338 Euston Road
London NW1 3BR

Wayland Australia
Level 17/207 Kent Street
Sydney NSW 2000

Produced by Arcturus Publishing Limited,
26/27 Bickels Yard, 151–153 Bermondsey Street,
London SE1 3HA

Series concept: Alex Woolf
Editor: Rebecca Gerlings and Jane Bingham
Designer: Andrew Easton
Picture researchers: Thomas Mitchell and
Shelley Noronha
Project Manager: Joe Harris

Photo credits: All images copyright of Getty Images
except from front cover, copyright of Bettmann/
Corbis, page 5, copyright of Bettmann/Corbis,
page 22, copyright of Corbis, and pages 30 and 40,
copyright of USHMM, Washington, USA.

A CIP catalogue record for this book is available from
the British Library.

Dewey Decimal Classification Number:
940.5'31811-dc23

ISBN: 978 0 7502 7898 0

10 9 8 7 6 5 4 3 2 1

Printed in China

Wayland is a division of Hachette Children's Books,
an Hachette UK company.
www.hachette.co.uk

SL001514EN
Supplier 03, Date 0713, Print Run 2813

CONTENTS

CHAPTER 1

THE ORIGINS OF THE HOLOCAUST

Between the years 1933 and 1945, members of Adolf Hitler's Nazi party murdered over 6 million Jews in a deliberate attempt to destroy Jewish culture. The name given to this atrocity is the Holocaust.

The Jewish people can trace their origins to the nomadic tribes of Arabia, while their recorded history stretches back for over 4,000 years. Under the Roman emperors, the Jews were forced to give up their independent kingdom, in the lands now occupied by Palestinians and Israelis. Following a failed revolt in 70CE, they began to spread out across Europe.

The Jews were not the only peoples to migrate across the European continent. Unlike other communities, however, the Jewish people maintained a distinct sense of identity, which kept them isolated from other groups.

CHRISTIAN ATTITUDES

Although Christianity had its roots in the Jewish religion, Christians were particularly hostile to the Jews. The Christian gospel writers claimed that the Jews had called for Christ to be crucified, and Jewish people were commonly known as 'Christ killers'. The Jewish practice of living apart from their neighbours led to their isolation in separate communities called ghettos. Beyond the confines of the ghetto, Jews were often forced to wear an identifying badge, and anti-Jewish feeling soon became deep-rooted. This prejudice was known as anti-Semitism, a term derived from 'Shem', the Greek name for the Jews. (Shem was the son of Noah, one

A carved scene showing the Roman victory over the Jews in 70CE. The scene appears on the Arch of Titus in Rome, which celebrates the triumphs of Emperor Titus.

of the Old Testament ancestors of the Jewish people.)

The first major outbreak of violence against the Jews took place in 1096, when Christian crusaders killed up to 8,000 Jews. These attacks were known as pogroms, and they were fuelled by powerful anti-Jewish beliefs. In particular, a myth emerged in the twelfth century that Jews were responsible for the ritual murder of Christian children. According to this myth, which was known as 'blood libel', the blood of the murdered Christian children was used in the Jewish Passover festival. The Jews were also blamed for the frequent outbreaks of plague that swept through Europe in the Middle Ages.

One of the major causes of anti-Semitism was a deep-seated hatred of the practice of money lending. Even though there were Christian bankers, people associated the Jews with money lending – a practice that was condemned by the Christian church. In fact, the Jews were pushed into money lending because many trades and professions were barred to them, and a class of wealthy merchants gradually emerged within the Jewish community.

In the thirteenth century, there was an outbreak of expulsions and massacres. Jews were driven out of England in 1290, and from France in 1306. Then, in the fifteenth century, they were driven out of Portugal and Spain. Many Jews found refuge in Italy and Bohemia (present-day Czech Republic), where they were made welcome, and their education and financial skills were acknowledged.

Jews were routinely persecuted by the Catholic authorities in late fifteenth-century Spain. Many converted under pressure from the Spanish Inquisition, but others were burned at the stake.

JEWISH CULTURE IN EASTERN EUROPE
By the end of the Middle Ages, Jewish culture had become concentrated in eastern Europe, and thriving communities emerged in what is now Poland, Belorussia, Ukraine and the Baltic countries. However, with the disintegration of Poland in the eighteenth century, many Jews found themselves contained and stranded inside the borders of the Russian Empire. Unlike the Jews of western

Hatred of Jews was widespread in nineteenth-century Russia. This illustration shows Jews being forced to stay in the city of Kiev.

Poland, these people faced harsh restrictions on their movements and on the places where they were allowed to live. In most parts of eastern Europe, Jews were given equal rights with other citizens. However, Jews still suffered persecution and pogroms in Russia.

Anti-Semitism in the Modern World

As the nineteenth century advanced, Jewish communities began to benefit from new ideas of social equality. In most parts of Europe, there was a gradual breaking down of the ghettos as civil rights were granted to Jews. However, progress towards total integration remained very slow. Jewish culture in central and eastern Europe was deeply conservative, and many

Jewish communities chose to stay rooted in their traditional parts of town. Nevertheless, there was a gradual increase in communication between Jews and non-Jews. By the dawn of the twentieth century, many Jewish people (with the exception of the Jews in Russia) had achieved success in the mainstream of European life.

Racist Theories

In most parts of Europe, Jews no longer faced persecution for their beliefs, but that did not mean that the deep-seated tradition of anti-Semitism had entirely disappeared. Many people in Europe still felt an enduring hatred for the Jews, which was often supported by false scientific claims that certain races were naturally superior. These racist theories had their origin in the second half of the eighteenth century. According to these theories, white western Europeans belonged to a superior race, while Semites (or Jews), Slavs from eastern Europe, Africans and Asians were all seen as members of inferior races. The race of white people known as Aryans was believed to represent the highest possible level of civilization and progress, and Germans were seen as the purest Aryans of all.

HITLER AND THE JEWS

When World War I broke out in 1914, Adolf Hitler was living in Vienna, earning a living by painting postcards and selling them on the street. He joined the German army, serving until the end of the war. The defeat of Germany in 1918 meant that the German nation had to agree to the terms of the Treaty of Versailles. This treaty demanded that Germany should lose some of its lands in Europe, as well as its foreign colonies. The size of the German army was restricted,

Adolf Hitler in army uniform during World War I. Hitler blamed the Jews for the war and believed that Jews were involved in a plot against his country in the years following Germany's humiliating defeat.

The Protocols of the Elders of Zion, a forged document, claimed to disclose secret plans by Jews to gain world domination.

and Germany had to agree to massive fines to be paid as compensation to the victorious nations. Some anti-Semites saw the harsh terms of the treaty as part of a Jewish conspiracy against the German people. Wealthy Jews in Germany were accused of investing their money in enemy countries instead of joining the German army.

These anti-Semitic opinions all rang true to Hitler, who found support for his beliefs in the Protocols of the Elders of Zion, a document widely quoted in the period following World War I. Although later revealed to be a fake, the Protocols were believed to be genuine by many Germans, who saw the document as proof of a Jewish plot to gain world domination.

According to the Protocols, a group of Jews had backed the spread of Communist ideas, in the hope that Communism could be used to destroy Christian culture. Many Jews belonged to the Communist party, and when a

Adolf Hitler is billed as the speaker in this poster for a Nazi meeting in Munich. By 1925, he had become a confident public orator, skilled in the art of addressing large crowds. He could rouse his listeners into a dangerously emotional state.

Communist revolution was staged in Russia in 1917, anti-Semites claimed that this was part of a Jewish plot to conquer the world. The views of anti-Semites such as Hitler were reinforced by events in Germany. Following World War I, an elected government known as the Weimar took control in Germany. The Weimar government included several Jews, and these individuals attracted the hatred of anti-Semites, who were quick to blame

The catastrophic drop in the value of the German mark in 1923 forced many shops like this one to close down.

the government for its acceptance of the crippling terms of the Treaty of Versailles.

In 1918 and 1919, Jews led two attempts by Communist groups to take over the German government. Members of Germany's powerful business class were afraid that a Communist government would take over private companies. Anti-Semites deliberately traded on these fears and blamed the Jews for the Communists' activities.

THE BIRTH OF THE NAZI PARTY

At the end of World War I, Hitler became a member of an anti-Semitic party. Within just a couple of years, he gained prominence and became highly influential inside the group, shaping it into the Nazi party.

Hitler saw the chance to act in 1923, when France invaded the Ruhr region of western Germany, seizing control of most of the country's coal industries and steel mills. The reason France gave for this dramatic move was the Weimar government's failure to make the large reparations payment promised to France in the Treaty of Versailles. France's annexation of the Ruhr gave rise to massive inflation in Germany. Within a few months, the Deutschmark, Germany's currency, lost almost all its value, and thousands of businesses were forced to shut down.

All these problems were turned to the Nazis' advantage, as they blamed the Jews for Germany's economic collapse. This was a clever political move, as it provided an appealingly simple explanation for what were, in fact, very complex problems. The Nazis also attacked the Communists, in order to gain the support of the German business class, as well as the many middle-class Germans who feared the Communists.

In 1923, the Nazi party encouraged a public uprising against the Weimar government. Hitler addressed a rally in Munich, and led a march through the

„WIDER DEN UNDEUTSCHEN GEIST"

This Nazi advertisement shows the first burning of books by Jewish and Communist writers, organized as a public event in Berlin within a few months of Hitler becoming chancellor.

The Enabling Law, 1933

In March 1933, Hitler held a general election, with the aim of gaining a majority of seats in the Reichstag. However, even though the Nazis won 43.9 per cent of the votes, this was still not enough to give him the majority he needed to pass laws. Hitler therefore proposed an Enabling Law to give him extra powers. On 23 March, the day the Reichstag met to discuss this law, the 81 Communist members of the Reichstag had either been arrested or were prevented from entering the building. In the absence of the Communist objectors, the Enabling Law was passed by 441 votes to 94, ending democracy in Germany and making Hitler a dictator.

streets. His hope was that the German people would rise up and declare that he was their new leader, but instead he was arrested, tried for treason, and imprisoned. However, his arrest and trial had the result of winning publicity for his arguments.

THE GROWTH OF NAZISM

Hitler was released in 1924. In the elections of 1928, the Nazi party only managed to secure 2.6 per cent of the total vote, but Hitler was still determined to pursue his dream. He began to reorganize the Nazi party, creating support groups in rural districts, where anti-Semitism was especially strong. He also targeted specific social groups in Germany.

One of his first moves was to found a Nazi student organization, known as the Hitler Youth. This was followed by a Nazi doctors' group and a teachers' group, while a cultural group was created with the aim of promoting German culture and language. The aim of each of these organizations was to gain support from a key sector of society. By 1929, there was worldwide economic depression, with the numbers of unemployed in Germany reaching 8 million. Hitler promised the German people that a Nazi government would end all political divisions and help to give back a sense of national pride to the German people.

In the two elections leading up to 1933, the Nazis failed to gain a majority of seats in the Reichstag (the German parliament), but they did manage to win more votes than any other party since elections had begun in 1920. Hitler was also backed by a small group of anti-Communists, giving him the support he needed to become the political leader of Germany. In January 1933, he was officially appointed to the position of chancellor.

HITLER'S LAWS

Once he was made chancellor, Hitler wasted no time in dismantling Germany's democratic system. Hitler also introduced a series of anti-Jewish laws, which were intended to exclude Jews from social and cultural life. Jewish people were no longer allowed to work in government or the law. Measures were put in place to stop Jewish doctors and university teachers from working, and dramatic cuts were made to the number of Jewish students who could enroll in schools and universities. There were public burnings of books by Jewish writers, and any Jews who had been granted German citizenship after 1918 (a total of around 100,000 people) automatically lost their citizens' rights.

The first concentration camps were set up in 1933. They were special

In April 1933, the Nazis imposed a three-day boycott on Jewish businesses and shops. They posted official notices outside Jewish businesses, saying 'Don't buy from Jews!'

This photograph shows a worker clearing up fragments of glass on the morning after Kristallnacht. In German Kristallnacht means 'crystal night'.

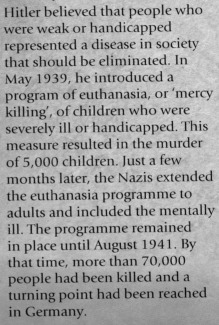

TURNING POINTS IN HISTORY

'Mercy killings'

Hitler believed that people who were weak or handicapped represented a disease in society that should be eliminated. In May 1939, he introduced a program of euthanasia, or 'mercy killing', of children who were severely ill or handicapped. This measure resulted in the murder of 5,000 children. Just a few months later, the Nazis extended the euthanasia programme to adults and included the mentally ill. The programme remained in place until August 1941. By that time, more than 70,000 people had been killed and a turning point had been reached in Germany.

prison camps where people could be held if they dared to oppose the Nazi party. The first prisoners sent to the camps were political enemies of the government, including Communists, socialists and trade union leaders.

From 1933 onwards, the Nazis rapidly stepped up their campaign against the Jewish people. Jews were banned from marrying non-Jews, and Jewish homes and synagogues were attacked, often by Nazi gangs. By 1938, one-third of Germany's population of Jews (originally numbering around 525,000) had left Germany, many

of them emigrating to the United States and Britain. In October 1938, Hitler expelled 18,000 Jews who had been born in the Russian Empire. The government confiscated all the property of the Russian-born Jews and they were driven across the border into Poland, where they were left to survive however they could. When the son of one of these families, who was living in France at the time, heard what was happening to his fellow Jews, he took violent action, shooting a German official in Paris. This act of passion gave the Nazis the excuse they needed to crack down on the Jews, and they launched the attack known as Kristallnacht; it was also often referred to as 'the night of broken glass'.

KRISTALLNACHT

On the evening of 9 November 1938, Nazi supporters took to the streets throughout Germany. Armed with sledgehammers and axes, they smashed and burned Jewish homes, synagogues and shops, littering the streets with broken glass. Many Jews died on Kristallnacht, and over 30,000 were arrested and sent to concentration camps. In less than a month, 1,000 Jews had been murdered.

The events of Kristallnacht marked a turning point in the Nazi campaign against the Jews. All over Germany, people had allowed the persecution of the Jews to happen, and some had even played a part in it.

Soon, the Nazi government had passed more anti-Jewish laws. Jews were banned from owning or running businesses. They were not permitted to use the sleeping or dining cars on trains; to visit public swimming pools or baths; to stay in hotels; or to attend schools, theatres or cinemas. The result of these drastic measures was to exclude all Jews from the social and economic life of their country. The Nazis also established an emigration office to encourage Jews to leave Germany, and emigrating families were carefully monitored to ensure that they left German soil.

The night of 9 November 1938, known as Kristallnacht, marked a point of no return in the Nazis' anti-Jewish campaign. More than 7,000 Jewish businesses were vandalized and 1,000 synagogues burned. Thousands of Jews were injured, and nearly 100 died.

THE HOLOCAUST BEGINS

This photograph was taken during the Nazi invasion of Warsaw in 1939. It shows Jewish men being rounded up by guards and marched through the streets to a concentration camp.

The German army invaded Austria in March 1938, and immediately declared it to be a part of Germany. Suddenly, 185,000 Austrian Jews were subjected to Nazi anti-Semitism. Jewish homes were ransacked and Jews were dismissed from government jobs. Faced with such persecution, Jews emigrated in huge numbers. Nearly 70 percent of Austria's Jews left the country in the months following Hitler's invasion.

The occupation of Austria was not enough for Hitler. One of the central messages of the Nazi party was the demand for Lebensraum (or "living space") for the German people, to enable the Aryan race to have sufficient territory to expand. In September 1939,

Hitler made his next move, and invaded Poland, Germany's eastern neighbor, triggering the outbreak of World War II. Britain and France recognized Hitler's ambition to control all of Europe, and were determined to stop him. On September 3, they declared war on Germany.

Once Hitler had gained control of Poland, nearly 2 million Polish Jews were at his mercy. He could treat them however he wished, without consulting public opinion as he still had to do in Germany. As his troops marched through the Polish towns, they rounded up and killed large numbers of Jews, as well as any non-Jews who dared to defy the Nazis. In the space of less than two months, 10,000 non-Jews and 5,000 Jews had been murdered.

The start of World War II and the invasion of Poland created a set of conditions in which the Holocaust could take place. As the Nazis took over more countries, they pursued a rigorous policy of persecution in their newly conquered territories. One result of the Nazi persecutions was a change in attitude by other countries that had previously taken in Jewish refugees. These surrounding lands, which were not entirely free of anti-Semitism, began to set strict limits on the number of Jews they were prepared to accept. Within a short time, European Jews became trapped in Nazi-controlled territory, with no possible avenues of escape. In this situation, Hitler's ultimate goal of wiping out Jewish life and culture escalated into an organized program of mass murder.

VOICES FROM HISTORY

Hating the Jews

Following Hitler's invasion of Poland, Jews had to endure violent anti-Semitism. One Polish Jew, captured soon after the invasion, remembered the cruel words of a German guard who noticed him resting on a cart:

"He made me get off the cart, aimed his rifle at me and bellowed: 'Du kannst laufen, Jude.' 'You can run, Jew.' He began pushing me towards those at the front ... constantly threatening to shoot me, cutting my coat with his bayonet. When the German cavalry passed us he pushed me among the horses so that they should trample me."

Dan Cohn-Sherbok, *Understanding the Holocaust* (Cassell, 1999)

JEWISH GHETTOS

One of the first steps in Hitler's program was the separation of the Jews from the Aryan population. In Poland, the Warthegau province in the west of the country became a part of Germany, and all the Jews living there were driven out. In other parts of Poland, Jews were confined to ghettos—areas surrounded by high walls—where their lives could be strictly controlled. The two largest ghettos were in the cities of Warsaw (the Polish capital) and Lodz. Jews in the ghettos struggled to survive. The Nazis kept supplies of food to a minimum, and anyone capable of labor was forced to spend their days building roads and army camps, before being returned to the ghetto at night. Nearly 30,000 Jews died of weakness and

SEUCHENSPERRGEBIET | OBSZAR ZAGROŻONY TYFUSEM
NUR DURCHFAHRT GESTATTET | DOZWOLONY TYLKO PRZEJAZD

SEUCHENSPERRGEBIET
NUR DURCHFAHRT GESTATTET
OBSZAR ZAGROŻONY TYFUSEM
DOZWOLONY TYLKO PRZEJAZD

The Nazis claimed that Jews carried diseases that could infect the Aryan population. This anti-Semitic sign reads "Infected Area." It was put up in a Jewish part of Warsaw, where people collected water.

starvation in the Warsaw ghetto in the second half of 1941. Inside the ghettos, the Nazis set up Jewish councils to organize work parties and other practical matters.

Jewish council members were usually picked by the Nazis, and faced a cruel dilemma. Should they cooperate with the troops or resist their demands and receive a terrible punishment? Once the Nazis began to transport Jews from other countries into the ghettos, life became even harder for the Jewish people. Entire families were forced to live together in a single room with little heat or lighting. Sanitation arrangements were completely

VOICES FROM HISTORY

Creating the ghettos

American journalist William L. Shirer, who was in Berlin in 1939, wrote in his diary:

"The Governor-general of occupied Poland, today decreed that the Jewish ghetto in Warsaw henceforth must be shut off from the rest of the capital... An American friend back from Warsaw tonight tells me the Nazi policy is simply to exterminate the Polish Jews. They are being herded into eastern Poland and forced to live in unheated shacks and robbed of any opportunity of earning bread and butter."

Martin Gilbert, *Never Again*
(HarperCollins, 2000)

inadequate and food was in scarce supply. Faced with these desperately overcrowded conditions, the Jewish councils set up their own police force, and sometimes treated their own people very harshly. While some Jews were forced to join the Nazis' work groups, rich people often managed to escape hard labor in return for large payments. Jews who could smuggle money and valuables into the ghetto stood a much better chance of survival than the poor.

They were able to buy extra food on the black market and even bribe their way out of the work parties.

More Invasions

As World War II took its course, the Jews of Europe faced an ever bleaker

Life in the ghettos was extremely harsh. People were forced to trade their most treasured possessions in order to buy enough food to feed their families.

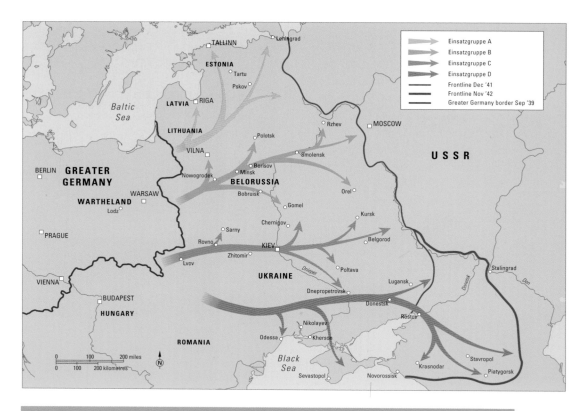

The Nazi Einsatzgruppen (murder squads) swept eastward across eastern Europe, killing Jews and encouraging anti-Semitic killings in Ukraine, Belorussia, Lithuania, Latvia, and Estonia. Jewish ghettos were located in eastern Poland, while the Germans took over western Poland and drove out all the Jews.

future. In 1940, Hitler decided to extend his power further into Europe. In the course of a single year, the Nazis invaded France, Belgium, Holland, Norway, Denmark, and Luxembourg, giving Hitler control of another million Jews. Many Jewish families who had managed to escape from Germany and Poland found themselves once again under Nazi rule. Jews in the conquered countries faced persecution and deportation to the Polish ghettos. Instead of simply driving the Jews out of Germany, the Nazis held the lives of roughly 4 million Jews in their hands.

Hitler's next move was to invade the

TURNING POINTS IN HISTORY

Stirring up hatred

As the Nazi murder squads advanced into Ukraine, Belorussia, Latvia, Lithuania, and Estonia, they found that many of the local people were more than willing to cooperate with them. The arrival of the Nazis unleashed a surge of anti-Semitic feeling, and many people helped in the capture and murder of their Jewish neighbors.

The overall commander of the Einsatzgruppen was Heinrich Himmler (in the center of this picture). Himmler also had complete control over German-occupied Poland.

This photograph was smuggled out of Germany to reveal the horrors of the Holocaust to the wider world. It shows Nazi guards supervising the mass burial of murdered Polish Jews.

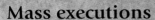
Mass executions

Hermann Grabe, a German builder who was a witness to mass murder by the Einsatzgruppen, described seeing a large ditch full of about a thousand bodies and the man carrying out the executions:

"He sat, legs swinging, on the edge of the ditch. He had an automatic rifle resting on his knees ... The people, completely naked, climbed down steps which had been cut into the clay wall of the ditch, stumbled over the heads of those lying there and stopped at the spot indicated ... They lay down on top of the dead or wounded; some stroked those still living and spoke quietly to them. Then I heard a series of rifle shots."

Dan Cohn-Sherbok, *Understanding the Holocaust* (Cassell, 1999)

Union of Soviet Socialist Republics (USSR). In 1941, Nazi troops began to advance rapidly into the USSR, followed by four mobile murder squads, known as the Einsatzgruppen. Each squad consisted of between 600 and 1,000 men, whose job was to capture and murder all the Jews they encountered. In every Russian village and town the death toll mounted until, by 1942, another 2 million Jews had become victims of the Nazis.

THE EINSATZGRUPPEN

The Nazi murder squads—known as the Einsatzgruppen—played a very important role in the invasion of the USSR. Their task was to eliminate all the enemies of the Nazi state. The main victims were male Jews, but other groups were targeted, too. Communist officials faced certain death, while gypsies and people who looked more Asian than European were seen as members of supposedly inferior races, and were often persecuted or murdered.

Most of the members of the Einsatzgruppen had been trained as policemen rather than soldiers, but the murder squads worked closely with the army. They also encouraged local people to express their anti-Semitic or anti-Communist feelings by organizing mass killings. The Einsatzgruppen adopted the same policy in each new area they entered. First, the Jews were separated into two groups—the strong and the weak. Those who were healthy and strong were put to work as slaves. The weaker Jews were driven into the woods. There they were forced to dig large burial pits before being shot dead on the edge of the pit, one by one. The formation of the Einsatzgruppen to carry out mass executions marked a key stage in the progress of the Holocaust. It was the first time that a systematic policy of mass murder had been organized by the Nazi government.

THE "FINAL SOLUTION"

The mass killings carried out by the Einsatzgruppen paved the way for the Holocaust. According to the original Nazi plan, Jews were to be collected into ghettos in Poland and then used as slave labor for as long as they survived. Following the invasion of the USSR, however, it became clear that this plan could not work with such large numbers of Jews. Sometime in the second half of 1941, Nazi leaders decided on what was later called the "Final Solution," or Endlösung. In the fall of 1941, Hitler gave permission for German and Austrian Jews to be deported to the Polish ghetto, and, by early November, approximately 20,000 Jews had arrived in Poland. Meanwhile, thousands of non-German Jews were murdered, to make room for the new arrivals. In

On January 20, 1942, a secret conference was held in this house at Wannsee, outside Berlin. The purpose of the meeting was to plan the genocide of the Jews.

TURNING POINTS IN HISTORY

The Wannsee Conference

In January 1942, important Nazi officials met in the Berlin suburb of Wannsee to make arrangements for the "Final Solution." They were told that the genocide of 11 million Jews was to be their priority, but other minorities, including Gypsies and homosexuals, would also be eliminated.

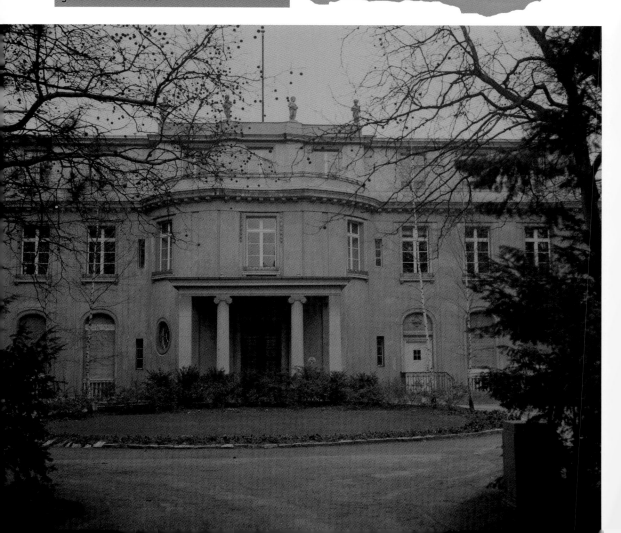

WHY DID IT HAPPEN ?

Did Jewish councils help?

According to Hannah Arendt, a German Jewish thinker, the Jewish councils in the ghettos made it easier for the Nazis to organize the Holocaust. "Jewish officials could be trusted to compile the lists of persons and of their property, to secure money from the deportees to defray the expenses of their deportation and extermination, to keep track of vacated apartments, to supply police forces, to help seize Jews and get them on trains." Arendt believed that more Jews would have survived if the Jewish council had been less cooperative and organized. However, Isaiah Trunk, who studied the Jewish councils, took a different view. He wrote that "the Jews were forced to establish the councils" and that "individuals were forced to provide services for the Germans."

Michael R. Marrus, *The Holocaust in History* (Penguin, 1993)

This photograph shows Doctor Josef Mengele, who was made chief medical officer at the Auschwitz concentration camp in May 1943. The Jewish prisoners called him the "Angel of Death" because he always wore a spotless white medical coat.

August, 1941, the Einsatzgruppen started to murder Jewish women and children as well as men. However, even this highly organized mass murder could not eradicate the millions of Jews. The Nazis now planned the complete physical elimination of all the Jews in Europe. No government had ever attempted the deliberate murder of such vast numbers of people, and the plan required the same efficient planning as an industrial process. A system of mass murder was developed, along the same lines as a factory program to mass produce cans or cars.

It was decided that the most efficient method of killing millions of people would be to use poison gas. By spring 1942, work had begun on a plan to identify every Jew in Europe. Once identified, the Jews could be deported to a death camp in Poland where they could be put to death.

CHAPTER 3

CAMPS OF DEATH

Six death camps were set up in Poland between December 1941 and the summer of 1942. Two of these camps—Auschwitz and Majdanek—were labor and prison camps with added gas chambers. Three more camps, at Belzec, Sobibor, and Treblinka, were constructed specifically for the purpose of killing Jewish prisoners. The Jews at these camps were never told what would happen to them. When new prisoners arrived, they were told they would be given a shower, and were herded into a special chamber. Then poison gas was released instead of water.

The sixth Polish death camp was established at Chelmno in December 1941. It was unique among the death camps in having special vans whose poisonous exhaust fumes could be channeled back into the interior of the van. The vans were filled with prisoners and driven to a local forest. By the end of the journey, all the prisoners had been killed by the fumes. Just a few Jews were kept alive, so they could bury the dead in the forest. Altogether, about 400,000 people were murdered at Chelmno.

AUSCHWITZ

After all the Polish Jews had been murdered, most of Europe's remaining Jews were sent to Auschwitz, along with many Gypsies and homosexuals. The camp covered an area of around nineteen square miles and was built on farmland outside the town of Oswiecim,

This photograph shows prisoners at Majdanek death camp soon after Soviet troops liberated the camp in July 1944. About 200,000 people died at Majdanek.

The six major Nazi death camps were located close to railway lines so victims could reach them in large numbers. All six camps were in eastern Poland.

Burying fellow prisoners

Some Jews were forced to help in the work of burying their fellow Jews. Yakov Grojanowski, who was held at Chelmno camp, had clear memories of what happened to him on January 12, 1942:

"That afternoon the work lasted till six. Nine vans, each of sixty Jews from Klodawa, were buried; five hundred from Klodawa in all. My friend Getzel Chrzastowski screamed terribly for a moment when he recognised his fourteen-year-old son, who had just been thrown into the ditch. We had to stop him, too, from begging the Germans to shoot him."

Martin Gilbert, *Never Again*
(HarperCollins, 2000)

called Auschwitz by the Germans.

When it was first created in 1940, Auschwitz was intended to be a labor camp where Jews and political prisoners were detained. Although some prisoners died there, it was not intended as a death factory. However, a second camp was built in 1941. Named Birkenau after a nearby village, it was equipped with three gas chambers and was primarily a death camp. Each of the gas chambers at Birkenau could hold over 1,000 people. The third camp on the Auschwitz site was a large slave labor factory run by I.G. Farben, a German

In April 1945, the British army liberated the Bergen-Belsen concentration camp. They found 40,000 bodies in mass graves, and thousands of unburied dead.

chemical company, and several smaller work camps, including a shoe factory.

Auschwitz was ideally situated from the Nazi point of view because of the railway links that connected it with other parts of Europe. Trains full of Jews arrived at Auschwitz, and the passengers were ordered to form two lines. One line was for strong and healthy men and women, who could be used as slave labor. The other was for older men and women, and children. A couple of doctors usually helped to make the decisions about which lines the prisoners should join. Then the older people and children were told that they would be given a shower, but instead they were led into the gas chambers. Most of them were dead within just a few hours of arriving in Auschwitz, and the bodies of the dead were burned in giant incinerators.

In the years that Birkenhau was operating, between 40,000 and 120,000 slave laborers lived in appallingly cramped conditions in 200 wooden huts. The camp was controlled by around 7,000 German guards, while the gas chambers were staffed almost entirely by Jewish victims, working day and night. The process of mass murder at Birkenau became increasingly streamlined, until in 1944 it took less than two months to eliminate half a million Hungarian Jews.

RUNNING THE CAMPS

All the death camps were run in the same brutally efficient way. The team in charge of the camp consisted of about thirty high-ranking members of the SS, or Schutzstaffel (German for "protection squads"). These men had originally worked as bodyguards for important Nazis. The ordinary guards were former Einsatzgruppen officials and men recruited from the local villages, and a team of about ninety of these guards was responsible for the everyday running of the camp.

In order to enable the camps to function with a minimum number of guards, it was necessary to keep panic to a minimum. At the railway stations, where the victims arrived in the

VOICES FROM HISTORY

"We didn't believe it"

Many Jews could not believe what was happening in the camps. Lilli Kopecky remembers her experience at Auschwitz:

"I recall a Dutch Jew asking angrily, 'Where is my wife? Where are my children?' The Jews in the barracks said to him, 'Look at the chimney [of the gas chamber]. They are up there.' But the Dutch Jew cursed them ... This is the greatest strength of the whole crime, its unbelievability. When we came to Auschwitz, we smelt the sweet smell. They said to us: 'There the people are gassed, three kilometres over there.' We didn't believe it..."

Martin Gilbert, *Never Again* (HarperCollins, 2000)

All Jews transported to the death camps had to wear a yellow star to identify them as Jewish. This group is shown on arrival at Auschwitz. Some were chosen to work in the camp, but most faced death in the gas chambers.

camps, efforts were made to make the places seem normal. Treblinka station even had a painted clock and signs pointing to a nonexistent restaurant and ticket office. The path to the gas chambers was lined by flower beds and covered by a tunnel of brush so that the victims could not see any bodies being carried away. The crematoriums were kept away from the gas chambers and hidden by trees. Victims entering the gas chambers were told that they were being given a shower, and were instructed to remember the peg number

Like Hitler, Heinrich Himmler was fanatical about the elimination of the Jews and the development of a master race of racially pure Germans. Here he is shown on an inspection tour of a Russian prisoner-of-war camp.

where they had hung their clothes so that they could collect them later.

In spite of all these attempts at deception, many people arriving at the camps knew what was going to happen to them. Faced with certain death, some prisoners panicked or tried to fight back. Others behaved with great dignity, and many mothers managed to stay calm, reassuring their children that they had nothing to fear.

THE SONDERKOMMANDO

Some of the toughest jobs in the death factory were given to the Sonderkommando—special groups of Jewish prisoners who were given minor privileges, such as better food, in return for their work in the camps. They had the job of reassuring the victims before they entered the gas chambers that they were simply waiting for a harmless shower, and some even worked as barbers cutting the hair of prisoners, apparently in preparation for a shower. Members of the Sonderkommando also had the terrible task of opening the chambers after each gassing session. Then, wearing rubber shoes and using water hoses, they had to wash down the corpses to make them easier to handle. Next, they had to tie strips around the bodies and drag them to the elevators that would take the corpses up to the crematoriums. At this stage, Jewish dentists had the task of extracting any gold teeth before the corpses were shoveled into giant ovens. Most members of the Sonderkommando only worked for a few months before they

Jews who boarded the trains to the death camps were told that they were being resettled. These Polish Jews, being supervised by Nazi soldiers, have no idea of their final destination.

became too weak to work any longer. Then they were also killed.

TRANSPORTING VICTIMS

Not only did the Nazis apply their planning skills to the management of the death camps, they also streamlined the task of transporting victims to the camps. The first stage in the mass transportation of the Jewish people took place from 1939 to 1942, as Jews arrived in the death camps from Germany, Austria, and Czechoslovakia. Jews were charged a fee for the cost of their transport, and were allowed to bring some possessions and food for the journey. The majority were sent to the Polish ghettos, but some arrived in Auschwitz, believing that they were

VOICES FROM HISTORY

Transporting Victims

Willi Mentz was an SS guard at the Treblinka death camp.

One of his duties was to shoot any Jews who were too weak to walk to the gas chambers. Here he describes his job:

"There were always some ill and frail people on these [train] transports … These people would be taken to the hospital and stood or laid down at the edge of the grave. When no more ill or wounded were expected it was my job to shoot these people. I did this by shooting them in the neck with a 9-mm pistol. They then collapsed or fell to one side and were carried down into the grave by the two hospital work-Jews."

Claude Lanzmann, *Shoah: The Complete Text of the Acclaimed Holocaust Film* (Da Capo, 1995)

Some of the tasks of the Sonderkommando were horrific. This prisoner was forced to manage a bone-crunching machine at a death camp.

This group of Jewish women and children has recently arrived at Auschwitz. They are awaiting the selection process that will determine whether they should be sent to a work camp or gassed immediately.

going to be resettled in eastern Poland. Once the Jews of Poland had been eliminated in the gas chambers, other Jews began to be transported across Europe to Auschwitz in special trains. The victims were packed into locked cattle cars without food or water. There was no sanitation, and barely enough air to breathe. The prisoners were in a desperate state. If they managed to spot a passersby, they begged for food and water, offering in exchange large sums of money and jewelry.

Historians disagree on the question of how much the ordinary German and Polish citizens knew about the death camps and the final destination of the trainloads of Jews transported through their countries. Some historians claim that thousands of people must have known about the Holocaust in order for the whole system to operate. Among these people would be railway clerks, civil servants, people living near the camps, ordinary German soldiers, and traders in the secondhand clothes that had once belonged to the camp victims. Other historians argue that the Holocaust was a well-kept secret. Even high-ranking Nazi officials, questioned at their trials after the war, claimed to have known nothing about it.

This photograph of the entrance to Auschwitz, taken in 1945, shows the railway lines that carried Jews to the death camp. Some of the victims' personal possessions lie on the rails.

THE BUSINESS OF THE CAMPS

Although the camps were run as death factories for Jews and other undesirable groups, they also operated as efficient businesses. Efforts were made to make a profit wherever possible. Gold fillings from dead victims were melted down and turned into gold bars, women's hair was shaved and used as stuffing for mattresses or knitted into socks, and victims' clothes and shoes were redistributed to German families who had lost their homes in bombing raids. Even the ovens at the death camps were designed to burn body fat, in order to economize on fuel.

In the larger camps like Auschwitz, prisoners with useful skills were put to work. Men and women under the age of forty who were strong and healthy worked as laborers until they grew too weak and were put to death. The camp hospitals were largely staffed by Jewish doctors, nurses, and medical technicians. Skilled metal workers, tailors, carpenters, and lathe operators worked in the camps' many factories, and musicians were forced to play in the camp orchestra to entertain the guards. Any man or woman who was not sent straight to the gas chambers was registered for work and given a tattoo on the arm with their number. Prisoners also had to wear a colored triangle on their clothing to indicate their status. Jews had yellow triangles and political prisoners had red ones. Green triangles were for ordinary criminals and pink triangles were for homosexuals.

As well as working in the camps,

Were most Germans anti-Semitic?

Author David Goldhagen has claimed that most Germans had strong anti-Semitic feelings. In his 1996 book, *Hitler's Willing Executioners*, Goldhagen states that it was easy for Hitler to bring about the Holocaust because of the preexisting "eliminationist anti-Semitism of the German people, which Hitler essentially unleashed."

However, many historians have disagreed with this theory. They point out that Goldhagen's explanation of the Holocaust is too simple and can also be seen as racist in its own way, because it blames ordinary Germans for the fate of the Jews. They stress that in 1933, more than half the German population did not vote for the Nazis, and many other ethnic and religious groups were murdered in the death camps.

David Goldhagen, *Hitler's Willing Executioners* (Abacus, 1996)

prisoners provided a valuable source of labor for German companies and businesses. Over fifty companies built plants outside Dachau (one of the original concentration camps in Germany) so that prisoners could be put to work. Many ordinary Germans also benefited from the Holocaust, as non-Jewish families took over the homes and jobs of the Jews sent off to the ghetto. There were plenty of people in Nazi-occupied Europe who were willing to take advantage of the situation. People knew that they were profiting from the suffering of the Jews, even if they did not always know the ultimate fate of their Jewish neighbors.

Jews arriving at the death camps were stripped of personal items of any value. This hoard of wedding rings was discovered in a cave near the Buchenwald camp in 1945.

CHAPTER 4

RESISTING THE HOLOCAUST

Anyone helping Jews hide or escape ran the risk of being killed by the authorities, but in spite of this, many people risked their lives to help Jewish people. They did this for many reasons. Some simply wanted to save others from a terrible death. Some saw the rescue of a Jewish family as a way of resisting Germany or the Nazis, and some were bribed by Jews to help. In Holland, there were riots when Jews first started being deported. In Denmark, a nationwide effort was organized to rescue the Danish Jews the day before transport to the camps was due to begin. In France, an underground movement was established to smuggle Jews to safety. Even in Berlin, at the heart of Nazi Germany, large numbers of Jews were hidden by their friends or disguised as ordinary German citizens.

Anne Frank was kept hidden with her family in a house in Amsterdam for four years. Her diary describes her life in hiding. In August 1944, the family was betrayed and Anne was sent to the Bergen-Belsen camp, where she died at age 15.

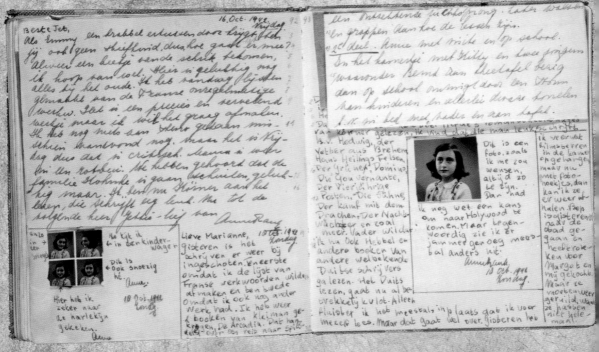

Some of Germany's political allies resisted Nazi demands to give up their Jews. In the allied countries of Hungary and Italy, deportations were delayed until 1943, and many Jewish refugees from Poland, Germany, and Czechoslovakia fled to Hungary. In Bulgaria, another German ally, ordinary people rose up in protest and put a stop to the transportation of Jews. Finland simply refused to give up its Jews, and Norway saved about half its Jewish population by ferrying Jewish citizens to neutral Sweden. China and Japan took in Jewish refugees.

Jewish organizations in the United States, Britain, and other countries sent cash to Germany and offered new homes for refugees. Meanwhile, Jews already living in these countries obtained work permits and visas for their relatives.

RESISTANCE ATTEMPTS

Many Jews preferred not to risk relying on others and took their own measures to resist and survive the Holocaust. Often, small groups of people in the ghettos decided to form resistance groups, even though they knew that their discovery would lead to almost certain death, not only for themselves but also for their families and fellow workers.

The majority of Jews in the ghettos saw resistance fighters as reckless and dangerous to the community. This was illustrated by a tragic incident in the ghetto of Vilna in Lithuania. Following the execution of more than half of the ghetto's 57,000 Jews, a resistance group was formed, which was later discovered by the Nazis. When the authorities

VOICES FROM HISTORY

Resisting to the End

A group of Jews in the Polish Bialystok ghetto managed to set up a self-defense organization. This is an extract from their call to action:

"Do not go willingly to death! Fight for life to the last breath. Greet our murderers with teeth and claws, with axe and knife, hydrochloric acid and iron crowbars. Make the enemy pay for blood with blood, for death with death! Will you hide in mouse-holes when they drag out your dear ones to dishonour and death?!"

Martin Gilbert, *Never Again* (HarperCollins, 2000)

demanded that the Jewish council hand over the resistance leader, the head of the council agreed to the request, probably believing that he was doing his best to save the lives of the majority of people in the ghetto. Many Jews hoped that if they did not resist they would not be killed and would somehow survive the Holocaust. However, this was usually a false hope. Not long after Vilna's resistance leader had been named, the Nazis took revenge on the whole community, killing all the Jews in the ghetto.

In a few cases, an entire ghetto acted together to resist the Nazis. In 1942, the inmates of the ghetto in Tuczn, Poland, were told to assemble at the

In 1943, the Jews of the Warsaw ghetto took part in an uprising against the Nazis. It was a symbolic act of resistance because they knew they could not succeed. Here, two resistance fighters are captured by German soldiers after the uprising.

ghetto gates the following morning. They recognized that this meant they would all be sent to a death camp and decided to take action rather than meekly awaiting their fate. In an act of deliberate defiance, they set fire to their ghetto, destroying the factories and anything that might be useful to the Germans. About 2,000 Jews escaped into the woods, though only a few of them survived until the war ended.

An estimated 40,000 Jews escaped from ghettos in 1942, fleeing into local forests. It was very hard to survive without food, and although some escapees were helped by villagers, others were betrayed by local people. Yet despite all the dangers, some Jews preferred to die in the act of resistance rather than be transported to a camp.

UPRISINGS IN WARSAW

By 1942, many young people inside the enormous Warsaw ghetto wanted to resist what was happening to them. This led to the largest act of armed resistance by Jews living in ghettos.

Gradually, the resistance group inside the ghetto managed to form links with supporters in the city. Over the course of several months, the group obtained a few handguns and homemade hand grenades. Then they waited quietly for the right time to

The two Warsaw uprisings took place in January and April of 1943 and involved about 35,000 Polish men and women. Here, an injured woman is being carried away after the fighting.

act, not wanting to invite punishments on other ghetto inmates. In January 1943, some members of the resistance group were selected to be deported to a camp, and the others decided it was time to fight back. The German guards were armed with automatic weapons and most of the resistance fighters were soon overcome. However, a few survived, barricading themselves inside a building. The barricade held out for three days, and twelve German soldiers were killed in the fighting.

After this first attempt at resistance, the ghetto returned to its usual routine for a few months. Meanwhile, the surviving resistance members had begun building hiding places and escape

This photograph was taken after the first Warsaw uprising in January 1943. Jewish resistance was brutally crushed by German troops, who used artillery to blow up buildings where Jews were sheltering.

TURNING POINTS IN HISTORY

Making a choice

U.S. president Franklin D. Roosevelt was informed about the death camps in Poland in December 1942. Several months earlier, Britain had been given similar information. Two years later, in 1944, the United States and Britain gained control of parts of Italy, making it possible for them to bomb Polish targets. However, they chose to bomb the I.G. Farben factory at Auschwitz, but not the Auschwitz death camp or the railway lines leading to it. If the death camp had been bombed in 1942, it is possible that the lives of thousands of Hungarian Jews might have been saved.

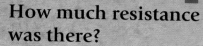

routes through the sewers. They had little hope for their own survival in the next battle, but they hoped that some unarmed inmates of the ghetto might be able to escape. In April 1943, the second Warsaw ghetto uprising began. Rumors had been spreading that the Nazis were planning to transport everyone from the ghetto to the death camps, so the resistance fighters decided to take a stand.

The Polish underground movement had been greatly impressed by the strength of the earlier rebellion in the ghetto, and they supplied the resistance leaders with two automatic weapons, rifles, and about 500 handguns. To this, the Jews added their own gasoline bombs and homemade hand grenades. However, they faced a very well armed German army. The Germans outnumbered the rebels two to one and were well armed with tanks. Nevertheless, on the first day of the uprising, German troops were driven out of the ghetto. Many had their weapons taken, and twelve of them were killed.

The April uprising lasted for a month. For most of this time, the German troops remained outside the ghetto, firing mortar shells over the walls. In the midst of the chaos, several thousand people managed to escape from the ghetto, staying hidden in the city until the end of the war. Many thousands of Jews were killed in the uprising, and all the resistance fighters died. The ghetto was finally razed to the ground the following September.

WHY DID IT HAPPEN

How much resistance was there?

Raul Hilberg, a Jewish historian, argues that the Jews offered no significant armed resistance to the Holocaust because they lacked a tradition of self-defense: "The reaction pattern of the Jew is determined by almost complete lack of resistance. The Jews attempted to tame the Germans as one would attempt to tame a wild beast." However, Yehuda Bauer, another Jewish historian, claims that the Jews did resist the Holocaust. He provides an account of a deliberate program of resistance: "It includes smuggling food into the ghetto, mutual self-sacrifice within the family to avoid starvation or worse; cultural, educational, religious or political activities taken to strengthen morale. The work of doctors, nurses, and educators to consciously maintain health and moral fibre to enable individual and group survival; and of course armed rebellion."

Raul Hilberg, *The Destruction of the European Jews* (Quadrangle, 1961); Yehuda Bauer, *Rethinking the Holocaust* (Yale University Press, 2001)

CHAPTER 5

An End to the Holocaust

By 1943, there was a sense in Europe that the war could not last much longer. Some prisoners in the death camps realized that if they managed to escape, they could wait for liberation at the end of the war. In August 1943, fifteen guards were killed in a breakout at the Treblinka death camp and 150 prisoners escaped, although some of them were later hunted down and shot. In October of the same year, 300 prisoners escaped in a carefully planned uprising at the Sobibor death camp. Around 60 of them were still alive and free when the war ended in 1945.

Also in October 1943, the Sonderkommando at Auschwitz rose up in revolt. This led to the destruction of one of the crematoriums, but prison guards shot nearly all of the 700 rebels. Some of the explosives used in the Sonderkommando revolt came from a

Roza Robota (1921–1945) was a courageous member of a Jewish resistance. She is pictured here in a group of prisoners—fifth from the left in the second row from the bottom. Robota was tortured by the Nazis after the failure of the Sonderkommando revolt.

Retreat from Russia

The greatest tank battle in history took place in Kursk, in Russia, in July 1943. The success of the German invasion depended on winning the battle. However, by the summer of 1943, the USSR had finally got its war machine into action and was prepared to fight back. Even though both sides lost thousands of troops at Kursk, the battle marked a decisive turning point in World War II. Hitler's troops began to retreat toward Germany, pursued by the Soviet army. In summer 1944, Soviet troops entered Poland and finally put an end to the Holocaust.

These Hungarian Jews are arriving at Auschwitz station in May 1944. The train journey to the death camp was terrifying, and anyone who tried to protest was shot down immediately.

nearby explosives factory. They were smuggled into Auschwitz by women factory workers and reached the prisoner Roza Robota. After the failure of the revolt, Robota was tortured. She was hanged on January 5, 1945, just a few months before the end of the war.

OVERCOMING NAZISM

Many of the ghettos of eastern Europe had been emptied by 1943, as their populations had all been sent to the death camps. Most of Europe's Jews were either in hiding or dead and the Nazis had begun the task of taking apart the ghettos, and destroying the evidence of what had been done. By early 1944, it was also becoming clear that Hitler would not be able to win the war. The countries opposing Germany—known as the Allies—were gaining the upper hand. Two of the allied countries, the United States and Britain, were preparing to invade northern France, while the USSR was ready to advance westward into Poland. Once they had reached Poland, it would not be difficult for Soviet troops to

A British soldier examines the incinerator used to cremate corpses at Bergen-Belsen concentration camp in Germany, soon after it was liberated in 1945. About 38,500 inmates were still alive when it was liberated, but around 28,000 subsequently died from exhaustion and disease.

fight their way into Germany. In June 1944, the Allies launched their D-day offensive on northern France and by September, about 2 million Allied troops were fighting their way across France and into Germany.

The Nazis found themselves trapped between two advancing forces. The American and British forces were marching from the west, while the Soviet army was moving in from the east. At the same time, German cities were being bombarded by massive air attacks. Faced with attacks on all sides, the Nazis made the decision to speed up the elimination of the Jews, rather than concentrating on the military defense of their territories.

THE HOLOCAUST INTENSIFIES

Even when Russian troops reached Hungary, the Holocaust continued in eastern Europe. In May 1944, the Nazis began emptying Hungary's ghettos, sending their occupants on trains to Auschwitz, one of the remaining death camps. These trains could have carried German troops retreating from Russia, and taken the soldiers back to the Germany, ready to defend their country. Instead, over a period of about eight weeks, the trains transported around 400,000 Hungarian Jews to Auschwitz, where they were gassed.

CLOSING THE CAMPS

Gradually it became obvious that the Soviet forces were advancing toward Poland. The Nazis responded to this by closing down the Polish death camps, but the camps did not all close at the same time. Belzec had been dismantled as early as December 1942, by which time most of Poland's Jews were dead. The Treblinka and Sobibor camps were closed toward the end of 1943, and by July 1944, a resistance group had taken control of the Majdanek camp. Auschwitz continued to operate until October 1944, but the Germans did not leave until January 1945, when they forced the remaining 60,000 prisoners to march through bitter winter weather into Germany. As many as a third of the prisoners died on the journey before the Nazis abandoned the survivors at Bergen-Belsen concentration camp.

Following the defeat of Hitler and the end of World War II, leading Nazis were tried in the International War Crimes Tribunal held in Nuremberg, Germany, between November 1945 and October 1946.

Will you speak out?

One very important lesson to be learned from the Holocaust is the importance of defending the rights of minority groups. The events of the Holocaust revealed how certain groups of people can be picked on and made to take the blame for events. In 1946, Martin Niemöller, a German pastor who was imprisoned by the Nazis, first spoke these powerful words, which have since been repeated in many different variations:

First they came for the socialists,
and I did not speak out—
because I was not a socialist.

Then they came for the trade unionists,
and I did not speak out—
because I was not a trade unionist.

Then they came for the Jews,
and I did not speak out—
because I was not a Jew.

Then they came for me,
and there was no one left
to speak out for me.

The Jewish Museum in Berlin is planned around an empty central space, as a reminder of the city's Jews, who either fled Berlin or died in the Nazi concentration and death camps. The museum was completed in 1999.

AFTER THE HOLOCAUST

For the prisoners who survived the Holocaust, there were many more burdens to endure. They had to cope with a future in which their families, homes, and communities had all been wiped out. Despite being liberated from the camps, they were still not truly free. Instead, they were moved to displaced persons' camps. Some of those who made the difficult journey back to their homes in eastern Europe were murdered by anti-Semitic groups in their old villages and towns. Between 1945 and 1947, about 1,000 Jewish people were murdered in Poland alone. About a million Jews had somehow stayed alive in the Nazi-occupied states of Europe. After the war, many hoped that they could build new lives in the United States or Palestine.

Jewish groups had been campaigning for the creation of a Jewish state in Palestine for more than fifty years.

WHY DID IT HAPPEN ?

Was justice done?

In October 1945, over twenty high-ranking Nazis were tried in the International War Crimes Tribunal. Most of them were found guilty. Some were sent to prison and several of them were hanged. However, some historians have questioned whether justice was really done. Many thousands of people took part in the murder of Jews and other minorities, but only a tiny number were punished. Historian Tim Cole argues that the extreme anti-Semitism that led to the murderous targeting of the Jewish people "received scant attention in a trial more concerned with crimes against peace, war crimes and crimes against humanity."

Tim Cole, *Images of the Holocaust* (Duckworth, 1999)

After the end of the war in 1945, there were suddenly thousands of Jewish refugees in Europe who had nowhere they could call home, and many of them dreamed of building a future in Palestine.

Gradually, pressure began to mount on the British, who were administering Palestine, to allow Jewish settlers into the territory. In 1948, Britain withdrew from Palestine, and the United Nations passed a resolution creating the new state of Israel. Suddenly, hundreds of thousands of Arabs who had been living in what was now Israel became displaced persons cut off from their land. This led to war between Israel and neighboring states. The Jewish people had begun a new stage of their history.

In June 2004, a ceremony was held to mark the opening of the museum and memorial monument in Belzec, one of the main Nazi death camps. During the ceremony, people lit candles to commemorate the thousands who died there.

HOLOCAUST TIMELINE

1215 Jews in Europe are forced to wear special clothing to make them easy to identify

1290 Jews driven out of England

1306 Jews driven out of France

1881–1882 Pogroms against Jews take place in Russia and Ukraine

1889 Adolf Hitler born

1919 The Treaty of Versailles punishes Germany for World War I with fines and the loss of territory

1923 Hitler helps lead an uprising in Germany that wins no support and Hitler is imprisoned

1929 Anti-Semitic groups formed throughout Germany by Hitler's Nazi party

1933 Hitler made chancellor of Germany

1935 Nuremberg laws deny German citizenship to Jews and take away their political rights

1938 During 'the night of broken glass', Kristallnacht, Jewish synagogues and other buildings vandalized nationwide and Jewish people attacked and killed

1939
September: World War II begins
November: All Jews in Nazi-occupied Europe forced to wear a yellow Star of David on their clothes
December: Jewish males, aged 14–60, required for forced labour in labour camps in Poland

1940 Jews are deported to the Warsaw ghetto, around which a wall is built

1941
June: Germany invades the USSR
September: Experiments on the gassing of prisoners begins at Auschwitz
October: The deportation of Jews to eastern Poland gets underway
December: The gassing of Jews begins at Chelmno death camp

1942
January: Wannsee Conference confirms plans for the mass murder of Jews

March: Transports of prisoners begins to the camps of Majdanek, Sobibor, Belzec and Treblinka
May: Gassing on a large scale in operation at Auschwitz

1943
January: German forces surrender to Soviet army in Russia
April: Gassing at Chelmno comes to an end
August: Gassing at Treblinka comes to an end

1944
May: Deportations of Hungarian Jews to Auschwitz begins
June: Allies land in northern France on D-Day; Soviet armies advance westwards towards Germany
July: Polish resistance group occupies Majdanek and Soviet troops enter the camp
October: Gassings at Auschwitz come to an end

1945
January: Soviet troops reach Auschwitz
May: Germany surrenders to the Allies
October: Nuremberg trials begin

1948 State of Israel established

GLOSSARY

Allies Countries at war against Germany in World War II.

anti-Semitism Prejudice against Jews.

Aryan The Nazi term for white-skinned Europeans not of Jewish, Slav or Gypsy descent.

Auschwitz The largest death camp built and run by the Nazis in Poland.

Belzec A Polish death camp where about 600,000 Jews were killed in gas chambers.

chancellor The head of the German government.

Chelmno A death camp in western Poland that used gas vans to kill about 400,000 Jews.

Communism The belief that there should be no privately owned property, and that an economic system needn't be based on profit making.

concentration camps Large-scale prison and work camps where prisoners would be worked to death.

crusaders Medieval European soldiers who tried to recapture the Holy Land in the Middle East from the Muslims.

euthanasia In Nazi terms, the killing of people believed to be of no value to society.

'Final Solution' The Nazi term for the complete extermination of Jews across Europe.

genocide The deliberate attempt to kill a people or a nation.

Majdanek A death camp converted from a former work camp at the end of 1941.

Mesopotamia Region of the Middle East, now Iraq.

Middle Ages Period of European history between the fall of the Roman Empire in 476 and around the middle of the fifteenth century.

Nazi Party Short for *Nationalsozialistische Deutsche Arbeiterpartei*, National Socialist German Workers' Party, led by Hitler between 1933 and 1945.

nomadic Not living in one fixed place.

Slav People in central and eastern Europe, including Russians, Poles and Hungarians.

Sobibor A Polish death camp that began operating in April 1942.

Treblinka A Polish death camp where about 800,000 Jews were killed.

FURTHER INFORMATION

Books:

The Diary of a Young Girl: Definitive Edition by Anne Frank (Puffin, 2007)

The Holocaust by R.G. Grant (Wayland, 1999)

The Holocaust: How Did It Happen? by Sean Sheehan (Franklin Watts, 2007)

The Holocaust: This is History by Christopher Culpin and Ann Moore (Hodder Education, 2003)

Questioning History: The Holocaust by Pat Levy (Wayland, 2003)

Websites:

The Beth Shalom Web Centre (http://www.bethshalom.com/)

A Cybrary of the Holocaust (http://www.remember.org/)

The Holocaust Centre (http://www.aegistrust.org)

The Holocaust History Project Home Page (http://www.holocaust-history.org/)

United States Holocaust Memorial Museum (http://www.ushmm.org/)

INDEX

Numbers in **bold** refer to pictures

EDUCATION LIBRARY SERVICE

Tel: 01606 275801

943